Für Walter Zöller
mit den besten Wünschen
zum 60igsten Geburtstag
von Kurt Ackermann
März 2000

Ackermann und Partner Deutsche Messe AG Expo 2000 Hannover GmbH **Halle 13 Expo Hall**

Ackermann und Partner

Deutsche Messe AG
Expo 2000
Hannover GmbH

herausgegeben von
edited by
Peter Ackermann

Vorwort von
foreword by
Sepp D. Heckmann

Prestel
München · London · New York

**Halle
Expo Hall 13**

Vorwort
Foreword

Der Neubau der Halle 13 ist das erste gemeinsame Projekt der Deutschen Messe AG und der EXPO 2000 Hannover GmbH.

Da die Einfügung der Halle 13 für die neu zu schaffende Südachse nach Vorgaben des Masterplanes der Architekten Arnaboldi, Cavadini mit Albert Speer und Partner von besonderer städtebaulicher Bedeutung ist, wurde ein beschränkter internationaler Architektenwettbewerb mit acht renomierten Architekturbüros als Teilnehmer ausgeschrieben.

Aufgabe des Wettbewerbs war, alternative Lösungsvorschläge für die Planung der Halle 13 und den Eingang West zu erhalten. Die Zielrichtung beinhaltete, zwei Nutzungen – sowohl für die Expo als auch für die Messe – optimal zu gewährleisten. Wesentliche Kriterien für die Beurteilung waren die städtebauliche Einbindung, Wirtschaftlichkeit im Bau und im Betrieb sowie vor allem das Energiekonzept und die Umweltverträglichkeit der Entwurfskonzeptionen. Die Ergebnisse, in denen sich eine intensive Auseinandersetzung mit dem Motto der Weltausstellung 2000 ›Mensch – Natur – Technik‹ widerspiegelt, sind überzeugend.

Alle drei Komponenten dieses Themas waren bei den Entwürfen für die Halle 13 zu berücksichtigen. Der Mensch soll sich in diesem Gebäude, das eine differenzierte Klimahülle darstellt, wohlfühlen. Die verwendeten Baustoffe wurden einer ökologischen Bewertung unterworfen. Regenerative Energieträger und die variable Nutzung des Tages- und Kunstlichtes waren weitere Bausteine der vielfältigen Vorgaben.

Der erste Preisträger, die Münchner Architekten Ackermann und Partner, hat nach Ansicht der Jury mit seinem Entwurf die Zielvorgaben optimal umgesetzt. Die Bauaufgabe barg einige Schwierigkeiten, denn es galt, eine Halle für möglichst viele unterschiedliche Nutzungen zu schaffen, die in ihrer Architektur zwar städtebauliche Akzente setzt, zugleich aber die schon auf dem Gelände vorhandenen architektonischen Schwerpunkte, wie Tagungs-Centrum Messe sowie die Hallen 2, 4 und 26, nicht übertreffen sollte.

Die behutsame Verbindung von Alt und Neu mit den zu gestaltenden großzügigen Freiräumen und der prägnanten Allee der vereinigten Bäume schafft eine urbane Gesamtanlage für Weltausstellung und Deutsche Messe AG, die eine gebotene Zurückhaltung mit städtebaulicher und gestalterischer Qualität verbindet.

Sepp D. Heckmann
Vorstand der Deutschen Messe AG

The new Hall 13 on the trade fair site in Hanover is the first project undertaken jointly by the Deutsche Messe AG and the EXPO 2000 Hannover GmbH.

The integration of this hall into the overall complex was of special importance in terms of the urban development of the new southern axis proposed in the master plan, which had been drawn up by the architects Arnaboldi and Cavadini in collaboration with Albert Speer and Partners. Eight leading architectural practices were, therefore, invited to participate in a limited international competition.

The purpose of the competition was to obtain alternative design proposals for Hall 13 and the western entrance. The overall aim was to provide optimal scope for two distinct uses: the world exposition in particular and trade fairs in general. Important criteria in the assessment of the jury were the integration of the scheme into the existing urban context, economy in the construction and operation of the hall, and above all, the energy concept and the environmental sustainability of the design. The outcome was a most convincing solution that reflected a detailed exploration of the themes of the Expo 2000: "Man – Nature – Technology".

All three elements of this motto had to be present in the designs for Hall 13. Human beings were to feel at ease in the building, and in this respect the sophisticated climate-control skin makes a major contribution by ensuring a sense of comfort and well-being. The materials used in the construction were subjected to an ecological evaluation; and the application of regenerable sources of energy and the flexible use of daylight and artificial lighting represented further responses to the many different requirements of the brief.

In the assessment of the jury, the scheme by the Munich architects Ackermann and Partners, which won first prize, complied with the conditions of the competition brief in an optimum manner. The brief itself posed a number of problems; for example, the hall was required to accommodate as many different uses as possible. In addition, the architecture was meant to strike a new urban note, yet not vie with the existing architectural highlights on the site, such as the trade fair conference centre and Halls 2, 4 and 26.

The sensitive way in which new and existing developments were linked with the broad open spaces to be created and with the striking Avenue of United Trees led to the realization of an urbane complex that would serve the needs of both the international exposition and the trade fair organization, the Deutsche Messe AG. In this scheme, the appropriate degree of restraint is combined with design and urban planning of the highest quality.

Sepp D. Heckmann
Member of the managing board of the
Deutsche Messe AG

Blick auf das Messegelände von Südwesten mit der Halle 13 im Vordergrund

View of the trade fair site from the southwest with Hall 13 in the foreground

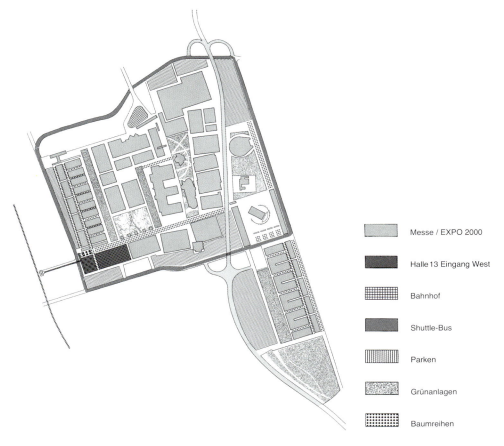

- Messe / EXPO 2000
- Halle 13 Eingang West
- Bahnhof
- Shuttle-Bus
- Parken
- Grünanlagen
- Baumreihen

Wettbewerb
Competition scheme

Der Eingang West und die Halle 13 übernehmen die Grundkonzeption und die maßstäbliche Höhenentwicklung der städtebaulichen Rahmenplanung. Die klare Anordnung der einprägsamen Gestalt des Eingangsbauwerkes und die streng geometrische, kristalline Halle betonen die Funktionsbereiche und stützen das städtebauliche Gesamtkonzept. Die Überdachung des Eingangs West und die Halle bilden den angemessenen Auftakt und gleichzeitig den Abschluß der Südschiene des Messegeländes.

Als Orientierungspunkt für das Messe- und Expogelände wird eine filigrane, transparente Dachstruktur vorgeschlagen. Über einen regulierenden Verteilungssteg werden die ankommenden und abfahrenden Besucherströme dezentral weitergeleitet. Die räumlich großzügige Anordnung ermöglicht Übersicht und Entflechtung der Funktionen in zeitlichen Abfolgen. Ein reibungsloser, kontrollierbarer Ablauf in den Ein- und Ausgangsbereichen ist gewährleistet.

Hall 13 and the western entrance to the site adopt the concept and the heights laid down in the urban planning legislation. The clear layout of the striking entrance structure, and the strictly geometric, crystalline form of the hall stress the respective functional purposes and, at the same time, reinforce the overall urban planning concept. The roof over the western entrance and the volume of the hall are the first impressions visitors have of the trade fair complex. At the same time, these structures represent the termination of the southern axis of the fair site.

A slenderly dimensioned, transparent roof structure was proposed as a landmark and point of orientation. The streams of arriving and departing visitors are distributed decentrally via a walkway raised over a broad forecourt. The generous spatial layout allows a clear view of the various functions, which are divided into a chronological sequence of discrete elements. In this way, it was possible to ensure a smooth, controlled movement of crowds in the entrance and exit areas.

A variable roof structure was designed to provide the necessary protection against the elements and to allow the area beneath to be used as a forum for a wide range of functions and communicative activities. The aerodynamic form of the entrance roof was meant to act as a wind spoiler that would increase the air pressure over the hall and thus serve the needs of the natural ventilation concept for the exhibition spaces within.

The restrained design and clear lines of Hall 13 lend it a striking, indeed unmistakable form. The principle of a hall that would permit variability in its layout and flexibility of use for staging exhibitions and trade fairs met all the requirements of the brief, which called for a space that could be adapted to a wide range of events. The logical, unspectacular load-bearing structure of the hall – free of intermediate columns – permits the internal space to be divided up in different ways, according to needs.

Wettbewerbsmodell von Südwesten, im Vordergrund das geschwungene Dach des Eingangs West

View of competition model from the southwest; in the foreground, the curving roof of the western entrance

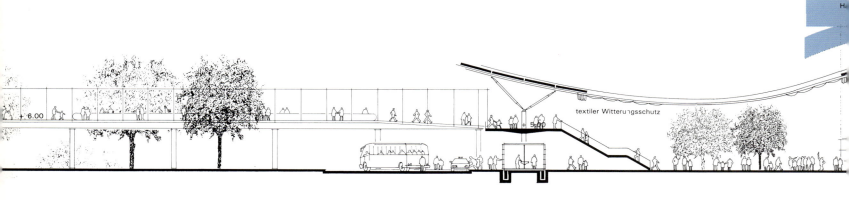

People - Moover zum Bahnhof Laatzen | Karlsruher Strasse | Bereich für Busse und Taxis | Umtauschkassen, Kartenautomaten, WCs, Kioske etc. | Vorplatz mit flexiblen Textildach als Sonnen - und Witterungsschutz

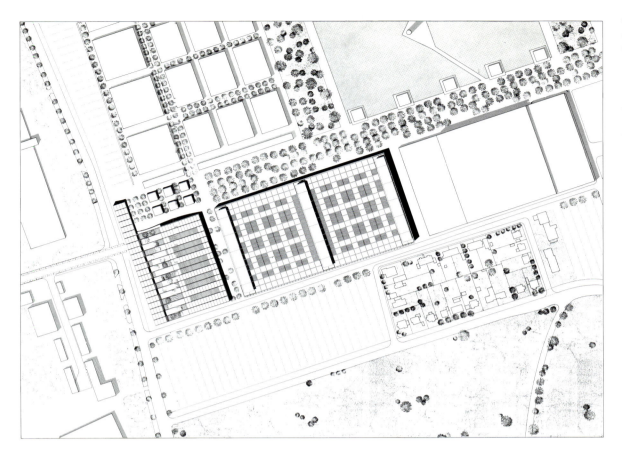

Wettbewerbs-Lageplan der Halle 13, ganz links der ›Skywalk‹ zum ICE-Bahnhof Laatzen

Site plan for Hall 13 (competition scheme); on the far left, the "skywalk" linking the fair site with Laatzen ICE railway station

Das veränderbare Dach bildet einen sinnvollen Wetterschutz und ist Forum für multifunktionale und kommunikative Aktivitäten. Die aerodynamische Form des Daches wirkt als Windspoiler und erhöht den Winddruck für das natürliche Belüftungskonzept der Halle.

Das zurückhaltende Erscheinungsbild und die klare Form geben der Halle 13 eine prägnante, unverwechselbare Gestalt. Das Prinzip einer variabel und flexibel nutzbaren Ausstellungs- und Messehalle erfüllt alle Anforderungen einer anpaßbaren Veranstaltungsstätte. Die logische und unspektakuläre, stützenfreie Tragkonstruktion der Halle ermöglicht die freie Aufteilbarkeit des Raumes.

The orientation of Hall 13 to the south-west – the main wind direction – led to a further technical consideration and the installation of the air-conditioning plant at the western end. The concept is based on the assumption that the natural wind pressure would be adequate to maintain the air supply and circulation for most of the time in which the building is in operation. The diagram illustrating this principle shows the relevant air currents and how the circulation works. Flexible fabric tubes, which function as fresh-air inlets, can be fixed to the principal air-distribution ducts along the long faces of the hall.

Schnitt durch den Eingang West und die Halle 13 mit der natürlichen Be- und Entlüftung der Halle

Section through western entrance and Hall 13, showing the natural ventilation system for the hall

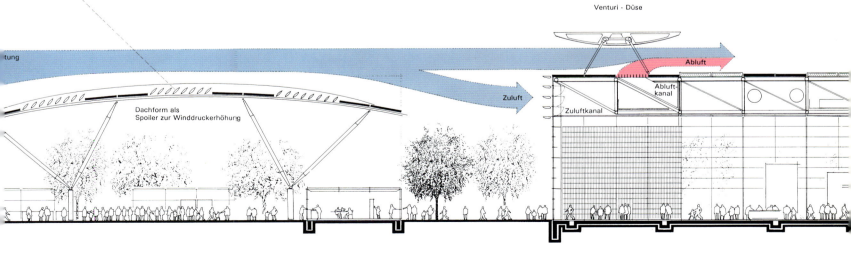

Sprengisometrie der Hallenkonzeption, rechts Belegungsmöglichkeiten der sekundären Dachstruktur

Exploded isometric diagram of the hall concept. Right: alternative systems for the secondary roof structure

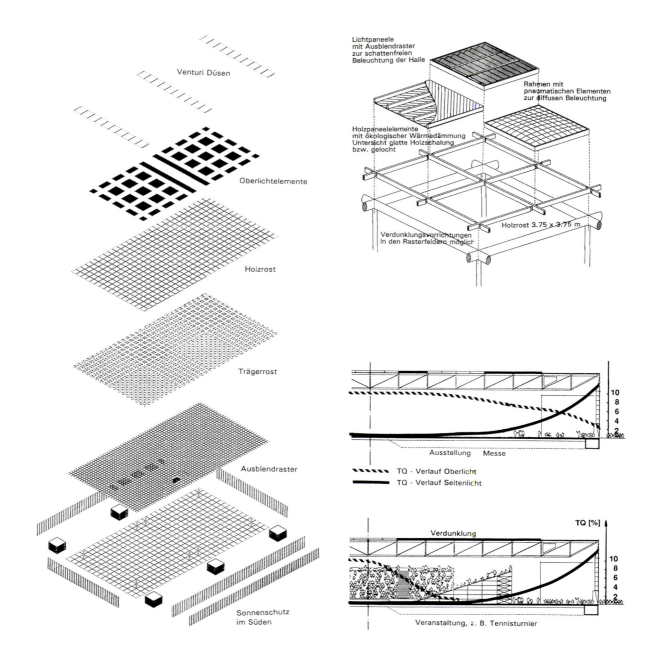

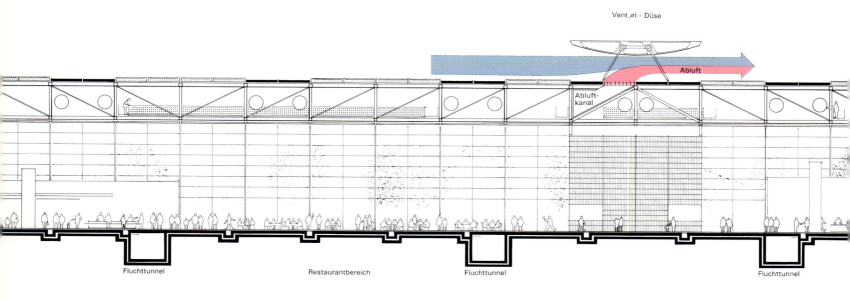

Die Lage der Halle 13 zur Hauptwindrichtung Süd-West führte zu der technischen Überlegung, die Anlagen für die Luftaufbereitung an der westlichen Stirnseite anzuordnen. Die Konzeption geht davon aus, daß der natürliche Winddruck in den meisten Betriebszeiten ausreicht, um die Zuluftförderung zu übernehmen. Die Prinzipdarstellung zeigt die Wirkungsweise der Luftführung. An den Längsseiten der Halle sind Luft-Hauptverteilkanäle angeordnet an die flexible Stoffschläuche angeschlossen werden können, die gleichzeitig als Quellluftauslässe funktionieren.

Im Hallenoberteil tritt die Zuluft gleichmäßig über die Fläche der gesamten Halle aus. Die Abluftführung erfolgt über die Fluchttunnel und Luftverteilkanäle, die auch als Medienkanäle genutzt werden. Die Abluft wird hier über ein Venturidüsensystem angesaugt. Der Lufttransport ist so konzipiert, daß mit geringstem Aufwand und Reißverschlußsystemen die Zuluftsituation dem Messebetrieb anpaßbar ist. Hier können auch vom Deckenbereich Zuluftschläuche in den unteren Bereich der Halle

An even supply of air is fed into the building at the top of the hall and distributed over the entire area. Exhaust air is extracted via the escape tunnels and along the same ducts as house the air-distribution and media runs. Vitiated air is sucked out via a system of Venturi nozzles. The air-flow concept allows the supply of air to be matched to the needs of trade fair operations by means of a "zip-fastener" system, thereby minimizing the use of resources. The competition scheme also provided scope for the installation of air-supply tubes that would lead from the ceiling down to the lower level of the hall. The air hoses were to function both as fresh-air inlets and as air filters. Depending on the degree of soiling, the hoses could be cleaned in a simple laundry process.

The tubular steel girder grid structure is based on a concept that allows the hall to be precisely attuned to different user needs and to be fitted out with media in all areas. The ingress of natural light, the artificial lighting system – which meets daylight standards – and the blackout installation can be individually controlled to comply with the many requirements made of the hall.

Von links nach rechts Schemadarstellung von – Abluftsystem – Zuluftführung und flexiblem Lüftungsschlauchsystem

Diagrams of hall services from left to right: air-extract system, air supply and flexible ventilation hose system

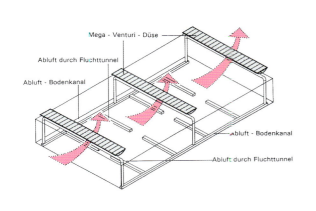
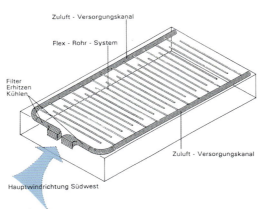
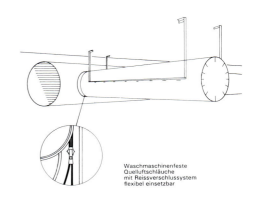

geführt werden. Die Luftschläuche wirken nicht nur wie Quellluftauslässe, sondern dienen gleichzeitig auch als Luftfilter. Je nach Verschmutzungsgrad lassen sich die Luftschläuche auf einfachstem Weg in Wäschereien reinigen.

Das Prinzip des Trägerrostes aus Rundstahlrohren erlaubt eine genaue Abstimmung auf die unterschiedlichen Nutzungen und Ausrüstung mit Medien in allen Hallenbereichen. Natürliches und den Tageslichtanforderungen entsprechendes künstliches Licht sowie die totale Verdunkelung kann individuell den vielfältigen Anforderungen angepaßt werden.

Die Optimierung des Energieeinsatzes erfolgt bei der wertvollsten Energieform, dem elektrischen Strom. Durch aerodynamische und thermodynamische Maßnahmen in der Raumlufttechnik kann auf ein mechanisches Lüftungssystem verzichtet wer-

An optimization of the energy balance was achieved by economies in the use of the most valuable form of energy, namely electricity. The application of aerodynamic and thermodynamic principles in the air-conditioning technology largely obviated the need for a mechanical ventilation system. Daylight was exploited in an optimum form by means of an antiglare roof-light system, which resulted in further energy savings.

The use of recyclable and ecologically sustainable materials wherever structurally and constructionally appropriate led to a minimization of the resources required for the building. The specification of timber – the only regrowable building product – for the floor

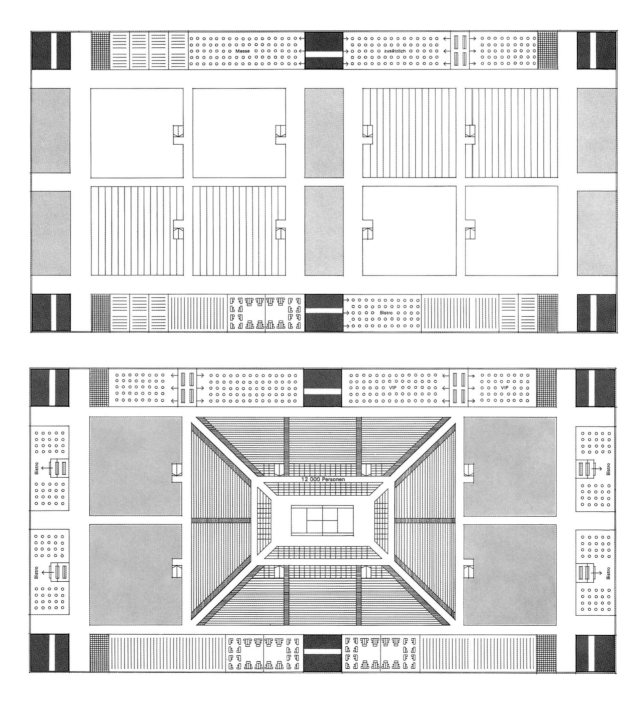

Geforderte Varianten der Hallenbelegung: oben Messenutzung, unten Tennisveranstaltung

Examples of alternative hall uses required in brief. Top: trade fair; bottom: tennis tournament

Innenraummodell der Machbarkeitsstudie mit Blick auf die Galerie an der Hallenwestseite

Model of interior for feasibility study with view of gallery along west side of hall

den. Die optimale Ausnutzung von Tageslicht durch das blendfreie Oberlichtsystem führt zu weiteren Energieeinsparungen.

Der Einsatz von recyclebaren und ökologischen Baustoffen für ihre statisch-konstruktiven Aufgaben führt zu einer Minimierung des Materialaufwandes. Die Verwendung von Holz – als einzigem nachwachsendem Baustoff – im Bereich Decken- und Fassadenkonstruktion sowie Innenausbau garantiert den ökologischen Umgang mit Baustoffen.

»Die städtebauliche Antwort auf die Aufgabenstellung ist deshalb optimal gelöst, weil Eingangsbereich und Halle eine ausgewogene und gesamthafte Lösung darstellen. Die Halle selbst fügt sich harmonisch in das Gesamtbild der Messe ein. Die Fassade der Halle ermöglicht einen intensiven Wechsel zwischen dem Innen- und Außenraum. Durch die sechs Technikkerne erhält die Halle eine hohe Funktionalität und klare räumliche Qualität. Diese räumliche Qualität wird durch das Tageslichtkonzept von Fassade und Dach deutlich verstärkt.«
Auszug aus dem Protokoll der Jury

and façade construction and for the internal fittings and finishings ensured an ecological approach to materials.

"The urban response to the brief provides an ideal solution. The entrance area and the hall form a balanced, unified whole. The hall itself fits harmoniously into the overall picture of the trade fair development. The hall façades stimulate an intense interaction between internal and external spaces. The six technical service cores lend the hall a high degree of functional efficiency and a clear spatial quality, which is further accentuated by the daylight concept incorporated in the façade and roof."
Excerpt from the jury report

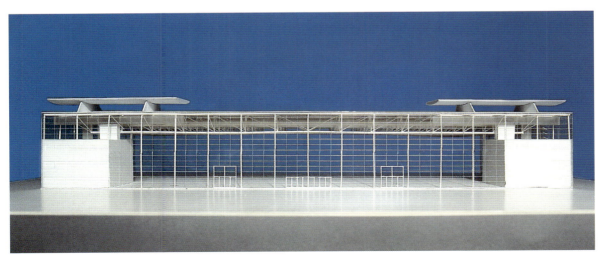

Modellaufnahme der Hallenstirnseite mit Venturiflügel

Model of end face of hall with Venturi elements

**Gesamtkonzeption
Overall concept**

Im Jahre 2000 wird von Juni bis Oktober in Hannover die erste Weltausstellung, die Expo 2000, auf deutschem Boden stattfinden. Das Weltausstellungs- und Messegelände wird für den Zugverkehr vom neuen Expo-Bahnhof Laatzen erschlossen. Über einen verglasten, 300 m langen Rollsteg werden die Besucher zum Eingang West befördert.

Dieser wird 1999 fertiggestellt, allerdings in einer anderen Gestalt als im Wettbewerbsprojekt. Der ursprünglich geplante wellenförmige ›Spoiler‹ war aufgrund der vergrößerten Besucherzahl von 12 000 auf 16 000 Besucher und der daraus resultierenden Veränderung des Zuluftkonzeptes in der Funktion nicht mehr angemessen. Über die neu konzipierte gläserne Eingangshalle West betritt man die Halle 13.

Die Kompaktheit des Volumens, die ruhige Kontur und die Ablesbarkeit der Konstruktion prägen die Gestalt der Halle sowie die Eindeutigkeit der architektonischen Haltung.

Die Grundfläche der Halle hat eine Größe von 27 400 qm bei einer Länge von 226,26 m und einer Breite von 121,26 m. Die Gesamthöhe der Halle beträgt 18,60 m. Die Nebenräume, Toilettenanlagen, Messebüros, Hallenmeisterei und Snackbars sowie die gesamten Technikräume werden in sechs unterkellerten, dreigeschossigen Stahlbetonkernen von je 15 x 15 m Größe untergebracht. Sie befinden sich an den vier Hallenecken sowie in der Mitte der Längsseiten.

Die Halle ist mit Ausnahme der sechs Kerne, des Ringkanals entlang der Fassade und der acht Fluchttunnel, die zur Personenrettung aus dem Innenbereich der Halle dienen, nicht unterkellert.

From June to October 2000, the first world exposition ever to be held in Germany, the Expo 2000, will be staged in Hanover. Access to the site for rail traffic will be provided from Laatzen, the new Expo station. Visitors will be transported to the western entrance via a 300-metre-long glass-covered travelator.

This will be completed in 1999, although in a different form from that foreseen in the competition scheme. With the increase in capacity from 12,000 to 16,000 visitors on any one occasion and the resulting changes in the air-supply concept, the wave-like "spoiler" roof originally proposed was no longer appropriate to the function. Visitors will enter Hall 13 via the newly planned glazed western entrance hall.

The form of the hall and its clear architectural concept are distinguished by the compact volume, the smooth, untroubled contours and the legibility of the structure.

The hall is 226.26 m long, 121.26 m wide and has an overall height of 18.60 m. It covers an area of 27,400 m². The ancillary spaces – WCs, trade fair offices, hall supervisor's rooms and snack bars, plus the entire spaces for mechanical services – are housed in six reinforced concrete cores situated at the four corners of the hall and in the middle of the long sides. The three-storey cores with additional basements are 15 x 15 m on plan.

With the exception of the six cores, the peripheral duct along the façade and the eight tunnels, which serve as escape routes for visitors and staff from the central areas of the hall, the building has no subfloor level. The trade fair stands are serviced with electricity, water, telecommunications and data facilities via media ducts let into the floor of the hall at 10 m centres.

Adjoining the cubic concrete cores at the north-east and north-west corners of the building are two restaurants, each of which seats 250 persons. The restaurants are supplied by fully equipped kitchens in the service cores. A gallery along the western face of the building between the north-west and south-west cores provides additional office space for the management of exhibitions and other events.

The main line of access for visitors to the halls is from the west. Access for exhibitors and supplies is via four vertical-lift gates in the north and south faces. Services and deliveries to the halls for trade

Nordfassade entlang der ›Allee der vereinigten Bäume‹

North face parallel to the 'Avenue of United Trees'

Rechte Seite:
Südfassade der Halle mit feststehenden Sonnenschutzlamellen

Opposite page:
south face of hall with fixed sunscreen louvres

Die Versorgung der Messestände mit Strom, Wasser, Telekommunikation und Datenleitungen wird über Medienkanäle im Hallenboden im Abstand von 10 m sichergestellt.

An den Betonkuben der nordöstlichen und nordwestlichen Gebäudeecke befinden sich zwei Restaurants mit jeweils 250 Sitzplätzen, die von vollwertigen Restaurantküchen in den Servicekernen versorgt werden. Die Galerie liegt an der Westfassade zwischen den nordwestlichen und südwestlichen Kernen und bietet zusätzlichen Platz für Büroräume des Veranstaltungsmangements.

Die Haupterschließung der Halle für die Besucher erfolgt von der Westseite, die Erschließung für die Messebeschickung über jeweils vier Hubtoranlagen von der Nord- und Südseite aus. Zur Andienung der Halle für Messen und Veranstaltungen können Sattelschlepper über Tore von 5 x 5 m lichter Durchfahrt die Halle ver- und entsorgen. Im Osten schafft ein gläsernes Verbindungsbauwerk die wettergeschützte Anbindung zur Halle 12.

Die Primärstruktur des Tragwerks besteht aus einem Stahlträgerrost mit einer Systemhöhe von 4,50 m. Der Trägerrost liegt auf den sechs Installationskernen aus Beton, die auch die Aussteifung übernehmen. Der Quadratraster von 7,50 m auf 7,50 m resultiert aus der konstruktiven und wirtschaftlichen Optimierung des eingesetzten Rundrohrmaterials. Die Sekundärstruktur besteht aus vorgefertigten 2,50 m auf 7,50 m großen Holzkassetten.

Über die Architektur der Halle 13 urteilte der frühere Expo-Geschäftsführer Theodor Diener: »Die Halle 13 ist ein architektonisches Projekt, das die Qualität des ›Normalen‹ in beeindruckender Weise veranschaulicht. Alles scheint sich ohne Leistungsgehabe zu fügen. Die Halle 13 ist ein bauliches Symbol des Einfachen mit der Qualität des Besonderen.«

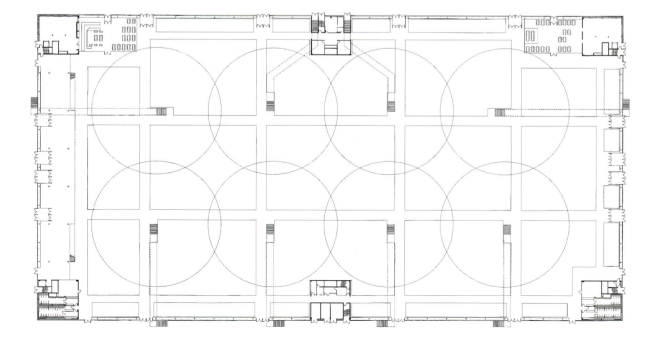

Grundrisse. Links Erdgeschoß mit Fluchtwegen, rechts Untergeschoß mit Flucht- und Versorgungstunnels

Left: ground floor plan with escape routes; right: subfloor plan with escape and service tunnels

Westfassade vor Fertigstellung des Eingangsplatzes

West face of hall prior to completion of entrance forecourt

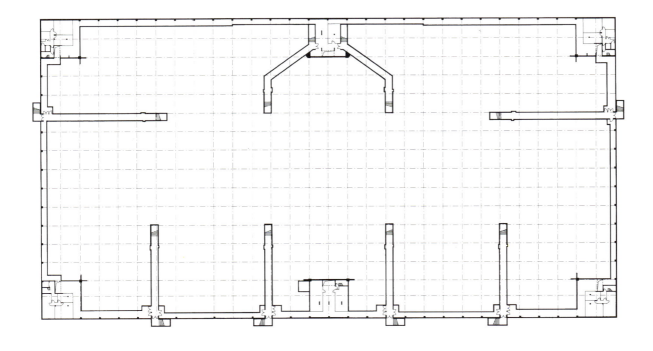

Längsschnitt mit der
Galerie im Westen

Longitudinal section with
gallery at western end

Blick von Nordwesten,
im Vordergrund die
›Allee der vereinigten
Bäume‹

View from north-west
with 'Avenue of United
Trees' in front of the hall

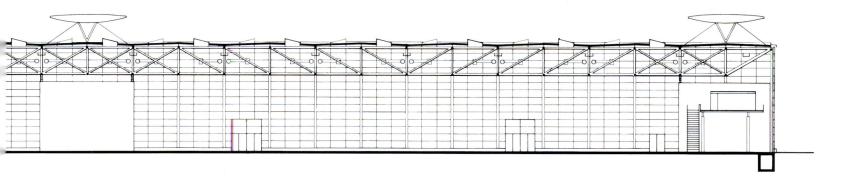

fairs and other events can be made by articulated lorries through gateways with 5 x 5 m clear openings. At the eastern end, a glazed linking tract was created to Hall 12 to protect visitors against the vagaries of the weather.

The primary load-bearing structure consists of a grid of steel girders with a system depth of 4.50 m. The girder grid is supported by the six concrete service cores, which also serve to brace the building. The hall is based on a 7.50 x 7.50 m square grid, the dimensions of which were determined by a concept of constructional and economic optimization of the tubular material used for the structural members.

The secondary structure comprises a system of 2.50 x 7.50 m prefabricated timber panels.

Theodor Diener, the former Expo manager, described the architecture as follows: "Hall 13 is an architectural project that demonstrates the quality of 'normal' things in a most impressive way. Everything seems to fit together effortlessly and without any great show. Hall 13 is a built symbol of simplicity that exhibits all the qualities of something special."

Westseite der Halle mit den Windfängen der Eingänge unter der Galerie

West face of hall with entrance lobbies beneath the gallery

Querschnitt mit der Galerie im Westen

Cross-section with gallery at western end

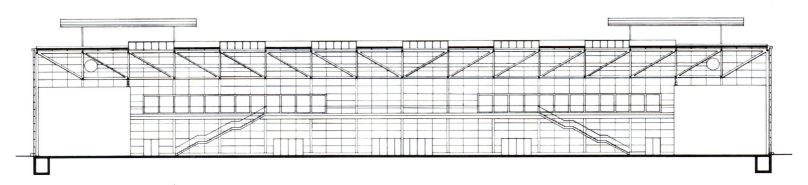

Büroboxen für Veranstaltungsmanagement auf der Galerie

Office boxes on the gallery for the management of events

Südfassade mit Hubtoranlage zur Hallenversorgung

South face with vertically lifting gate for servicing hall

**Termine/Planung/ Bauablauf
Deadlines/Planning/ Construction sequence**

Das Bauwerk wurde nach einem getakteten Ablauf von der Mitte der Halle in östlicher und in westlicher Richtung erstellt. Die Betonkuben der Servicebauwerke wurden vorab errichtet, dann wurden die Sohlbereiche betoniert. Die 10,90 m hohen Sichtbetonwände der Servicekerne wurden in einem Betonierabschnitt gegossen. Der gesamte Rohbau wurde in der Rekordzeit von drei Monaten von November bis Januar abgewickelt.

Die biegesteife Stahlkonstruktion ergab für die Montage folgenden Ablauf: Einzelschüsse der Hallenquerrichtung von 30 m wurden in der Werkstatt in der vorgesehenen überhöhten Geometrie vorgefertigt. Auf Rüsttürmen im Rastermaß von 30 x 30 m sind diese Segmente kammartig vorgebaut und untereinander verschweißt worden. Die fehlenden Gurte und Diagonalen der Träger in Hallenlängsrichtung wurden sukzessive ergänzt. Gemäß dem Betonbau erfolgte der Weiterbau jeweils zeitversetzt nach Ost und West. Die Fassadenstützen wurden gleichzeitig eingebaut, so daß die Pfosten-Riegel-Konstruktion der Fassade ohne Verzögerung montiert werden konnte. Sobald die ersten Felder des Stahlbaues freigegeben waren, folgte das Auflegen der Holzelemente der Dachkonstruktion. Nach der vollständigen Verschweißung aller Verbindungen wurde der Trägerrost mittels hydraulischer Pressen abgesenkt, auf die Innenecken der Betontürme aufgelegt und in sein Eigengewicht entlassen. Die Bauzeit der Gesamtkonstruktion betrug 10 Monate – vom Oktober '96 bis Juli '97. Mit der ATP-Tennisweltmeisterschaft 1997 wurde die neue Halle 13 der Deutschen Messe in Hannover offiziell eröffnet.

The building was constructed in a regular phased sequence from the centre outwards, working towards the east and west. The concrete cubic structures that house the services were the first elements to be erected. The 10.90-metre-high exposed concrete walls to the service cores were poured in a single sequence. This phase of the work was followed by the concreting of the substructure and base slab. The entire carcass structure was completed in a record time of three months, from November to January.

The flexurally rigid steel structure was manufactured and assembled in the following stages. Individual 30-metre segments to be erected across the width of the hall were prefabricated at works with an inbuilt hogged geometry. The segments were then pre-assembled in a comb-like form and welded together on scaffolding towers laid out at 30 x 30 m centres. The missing links – the chords and diagonals in the longitudinal direction of the girder grid – were then added successively. Following the execution of the concrete work, further construction was carried out in the appropriate sequence, working in an easterly and westerly direction. The peripheral columns were erected at the same time, so that the post-and-rail façade could also be assembled without delay. As soon as the first bays of the steel structure had been approved and accepted, the timber roof elements were laid in position. After all connections had been welded, the girder grid was lowered by hydraulic jacks onto the inner corners of the concrete towers, and the natural flow of forces took effect. The construction time for the entire development was 10 months: from October 1996 to July 1997. The new Hall 13 of the Deutsche Messe AG, the German trade fair organization in Hanover, was officially inaugurated with the ATP World Tennis Championship 1997.

Luftaufnahme der Baustelle von Südwesten

Aerial view of construction site from south-west

Rechte Seite:
Blick auf einen Mittelkern mit den Auflagerpunkten des Dachtragwerks

Opposite page:
View of one of the middle cores with roof structure supported on top

Haupttermine der Planung und Ausführung	1995							1996												1997											
	April	Mai	Juni	Juli	Aug.	Sept.	Okt.	Nov.	Dez.	Jan.	Feb.	März	April	Mai	Juni	Juli	Aug.	Sept.	Okt.	Nov.	Dez.	Jan.	Feb.	März	April	Mai	Juni	Juli	Aug.	Sept.	Okt.	Nov.	Dez.
Wettbewerb			▓	▓																													
Machbarkeitsstudie									▓	▓																							
Entwurfs- und Genehmigungsplanung												▓	▓	▓	▓	▓	▓																
Werkplanung, Statik, Haustechnik													▓	▓	▓	▓	▓	▓	▓	▓	▓	▓	▓	▓	▓								
Ausschreibung und Vergabe														▓	▓	▓	▓	▓	▓	▓	▓	▓	▓	▓	▓								
Baustelleneinrichtung, Gründung																▓	▓	▓	▓														
Rohbau Bodenplatte, Kerne und Kanäle																	▓	▓	▓	▓	▓	▓											
Stahlbau																			▓	▓	▓	▓	▓	▓									
Dacheindeckung, Oberlichter																					▓	▓	▓	▓	▓								
Fassadenbau und Verglasung																						▓	▓	▓	▓	▓	▓						
Technischer Ausbau																							▓	▓	▓	▓	▓	▓					
Innenausbau und Einbauten																									▓	▓	▓	▓	▓				
Außenanlagen																												▓	▓	▓			
Einweihung mit ATP-Turnier																														▓			

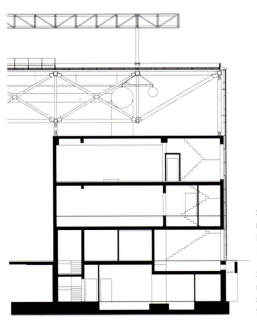

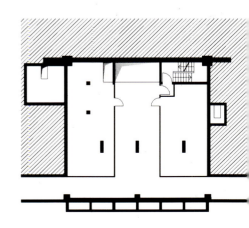

Schnitt und Grundrisse des südlichen Mittelkerns; UG, EG, 1. und 2. OG

Section and plans of middle core (south face); subfloor, ground floor, first and second floors

Schalarbeiten für die Galerie. 11 m hohe Schalung der Servicekerne

Laying shuttering for gallery. Shuttering for service core (11 m high)

Bereitstellung der Stahlträger in 30 m Schüssen. Knotenverschweißung in 17 m Höhe

Preparation of roof girders in 30-metre lengths. Welding node connections 17 m above ground

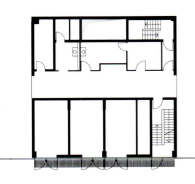
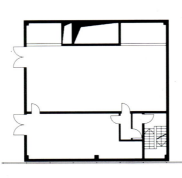

Tragwerk
Load-bearing structure

Ein über die gesamte Fläche frei spannender Rost aus sich kreuzenden Fachwerkträgern bildet das Stahltragwerk des Daches. Es wurde mit Holzkastenelementen eingedeckt, die auf der Obergurtebene im Gefälle aufgeständert sind und das Trägerraster von 7,5 m überbrücken.

Für das flächige Tragwerk wurde eine Kombination aus Linien- und Punktlagerung gewählt. Es liegt an acht Punkten auf den Innenecken der untergestellten Servicekerne aus Ortbeton auf und gibt dort seine Hauptlast (bis zu 1100 Tonnen) ab. Zusätzlich tragen es die Fassadenstützen. Aus dieser Kombination ergibt sich eine Einspannwirkung im Bereich der Eck- beziehungsweise Mittelkerne.

Das Dachtragwerk besteht aus warmgefertigten Rohren, St 52-3. Die Obergurte werden im Feldbereich vorwiegend auf Druck beansprucht, im Bereich der Einspannung über den Servicekernen vorwiegend auf Zug, die Untergurte in den Feldbereichen auf Zug und im Lagerbereich auf Druck. Durchmesser und Wandstärken der Rohre wurden der Belastungssituation angepaßt. Die Diagonalen werden im Bereich der Einspannung sowohl auf Zug als auch auf Druck belastet. Im direkten Lagerbereich sind sie kreuzweise miteinander verbunden, um die Lastabtragung auf Zug und Druck zu verteilen. Dabei stützt die unter Zugkraft stehende Diagonale die Druckdiagonale, beziehungsweise setzt deren Knicklänge herab.

Die Tragwerksteile sind in den Systemknoten über Gußelemente GS 18 NiMoCr 3 6 biegesteif zusammengefügt. Der Vorteil der Gußherstellung – Teilformen werden zu Gesamtformen zusammengesetzt – wurde genutzt, um für die Knotenpunkte ein Baukastensystem zu entwickeln. Mit Grundkörpern und verschiedenartigen Anbauteilen ermöglicht dies beliebige Anschlußsituationen für Diagonalen oder Pfostenanschlüsse.

Die Windlasten werden über geneigte Zug- beziehungsweise Druckelemente auf die massiven Kerne übertragen. Das biegesteife Tragwerk wurde für eine zusätzliche Schneelast um bis zu 500 mm überhöht. Unter seiner Vollast, die eine vertikale Verformung bis zu 300 mm ergibt, verbleibt eine Restüberhöhung von etwa 200 mm, damit ein ›optisches‹ Durchhängen der Konstruktion vermieden wird.

Sven Plieninger

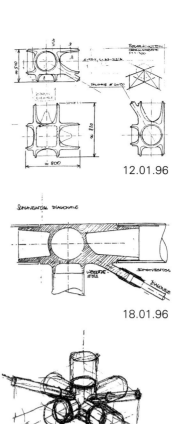

12.01.96

18.01.96

18.01.96

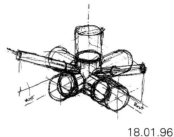

22.04.96

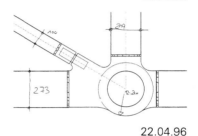

30.04.96

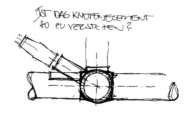

01.05.96

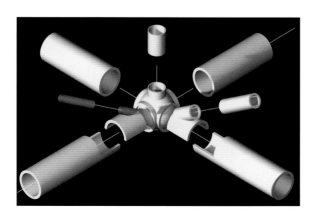

Entwicklungsstufen zur Formfindung der gußeisernen Verbindungsknoten. Computeranimation des ausgeführten Knotens

Design stages in development of cast-iron connecting nodes. Computer animation of the nodes as executed

Systemdarstellung des
Dachtragwerks mit den
acht Auflagerpunkten

Diagram of structural
roof system showing
the eight bearing points
on the cores

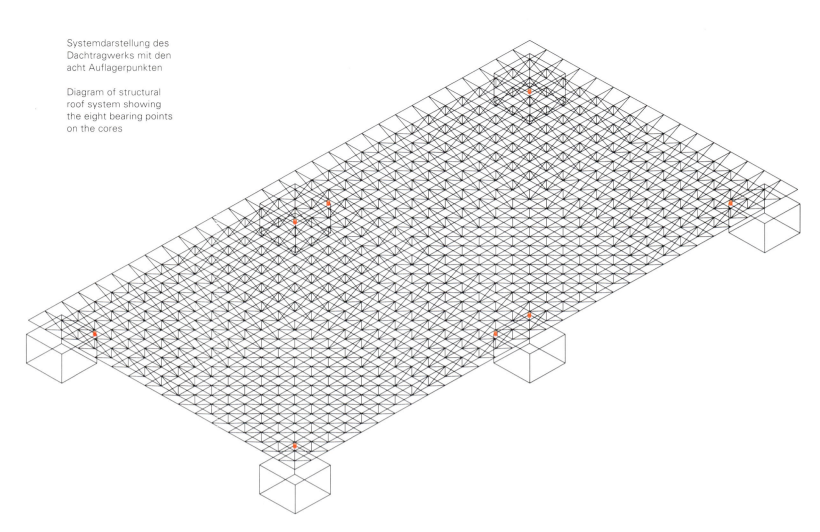

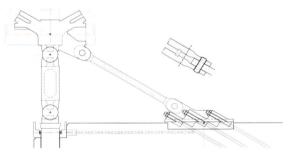

Auflagerpunkt des
Mittelkerns mit Quer-
aussteifung;
unten: Systematik der
Aussteifung

Roof structure support
on middle core with
transverse bracing.
Bottom: bracing system

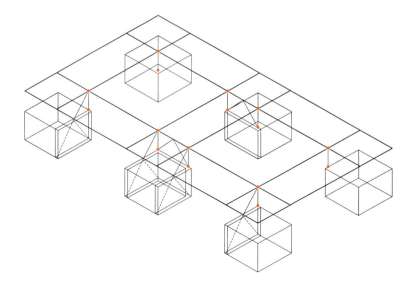

The load-bearing roof structure consists of a grid of intersecting trussed steel girders that extends over the entire area of the hall without intermediate columns. The roof was covered with timber elements that span the 7.5-metre dimension of the structural grid and are laid across the upper chords of the girders. The planar roof structure was designed with a combination of linear and point supports. It bears at eight points on the inner corners of the in-situ concrete service cores, where the main loading (up to 1,100 tonnes) is transmitted. Further loads are borne by the façade columns. This combination results in a restraining effect in the areas of the corner and middle cores. The roof structure was assembled from hot-drawn tubes (52-3 steel). The upper chords of the girders are subject mainly to compression stresses within the bays and tension stresses at the points of fixing over the cores. The lower chords are subject to tension stresses within the bays and compression stresses at the points of support. The various strengths of the tubes were determined according to the loading in individual positions. The diagonal members are subject to both tensile and compression stresses at the points of fixing. Intersecting connections between the members at the points of support serve to divide the loading into tensile and compression stresses. The diagonal members subject to tensile stresses support the compression diagonals. The load-bearing members are rigidly connected at the node points of the system by means of cast elements (18 NiMoCr 3 6). The advantage of the casting process is that individ-

Dachtragwerk mit Holzkassettendecke und Oberlichtern

Roof structure with timber panel covering and roof lights

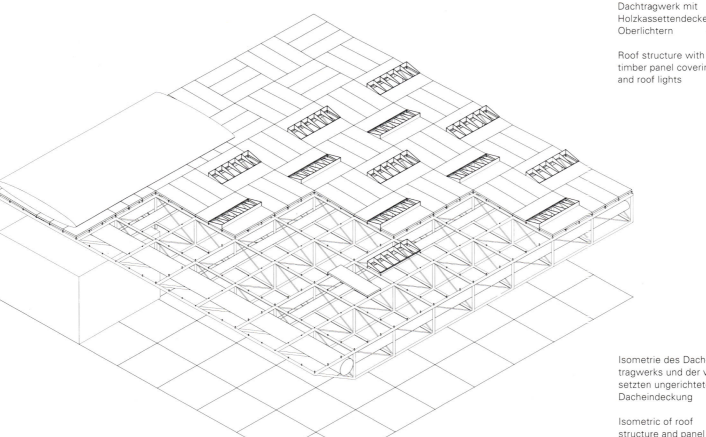

Isometrie des Dachtragwerks und der versetzten ungerichteten Dacheindeckung

Isometric of roof structure and panel coverings set at right angles to each other from bay to bay

ual components can be combined into composite elements. This allowed the nodes to be designed as part of a unit construction system. By combining basic components with various extension pieces, it was possible to create connections between diagonal members or posts in any situation.

Wind loads are transmitted via raking tension or compression members to the solid cores. The flexurally rigid roof structure was designed in a hogged form to bear an additional snow load of up to 500 mm. Full loading over the entire area would result in vertical deformation of up to 300 mm, leaving a residual hogging of 200 mm, which would obviate any visual sensation of sagging.

Sven Plieninger

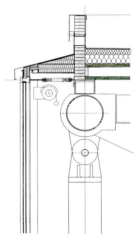

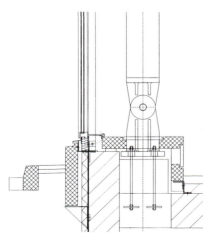

Schnitt Fassadenstütze und Sockeldetail mit den Lüftungsöffnungen für die Abluftabsaugung

Section through façade column and detail of plinth with outlets for suction removal of vitiated air

Fassade
Façade

Die Fassade ist als Pfosten-Riegel-Fassade aus offenen, thermisch getrennten Stahlprofilen konstruiert. Das Konstruktionsraster von 7,50 m wurde dreigeteilt, so daß jeweils im Abstand von 2,50 m ein vertikaler Fassadenpfosten steht. Die horizontale Teilung der Fassade beträgt 1,25 m, somit ergibt sich ein Fassadenraster von 2,50 x 1,25 m.

Die 17,50 m hohe Fassade ist für ihre Eigenlasten selbsttragend. Für die vertikalen Pfosten wurden filigrane T-Profile 60/90 mm verwendet. Die horizontalen, 7,50 m spannenden Riegel, dem Kraftfluß entsprechend als ›Eisenbahnprofil‹ ausgebildet, tragen die Windlasten zu den Fassadenstützen, wo sie dann zum Dach und der Sohle anteilig weitergeleitet werden.

The façade was designed as a post-and-rail construction, with open, thermally separated steel sections. The 7.50-metre bays of the structural grid were subdivided into three sections, with posts at 2.50-metre centres. The vertical divisions of the façade are based on a dimension of 1.25 m. The grid dimensions of the outer skin are, therefore, 2.50 x 1.25 m.

The façade is 17.50 m high and is self-supporting as far as its dead weight is concerned. The posts consist of slenderly dimensioned 60/90 mm T-sections. The horizontal members, which span a width

Fassadenstudie am Arbeitsmodell.
Rechts: Vertikalschnitt durch die Fassade mit ›Eisenbahnprofil‹.

Working model of section of façade.
Right: vertical section through façade showing 'railway line' glazing rail

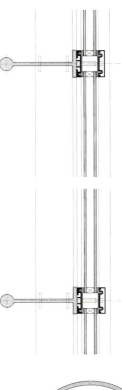

Horizontalschnitt durch die Fassade im Bereich der Dehnfuge am Kern

Horizontal section through façade showing expansion joint at service core

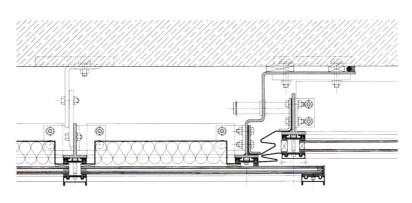

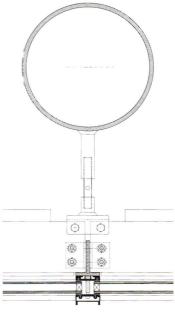

Detailansicht der mit 15°
geneigten Sonnenschutz-
lamellen

Detail of louvres inclined
at 15°

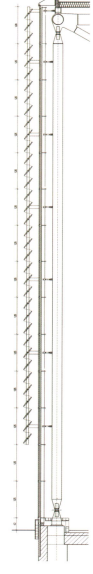
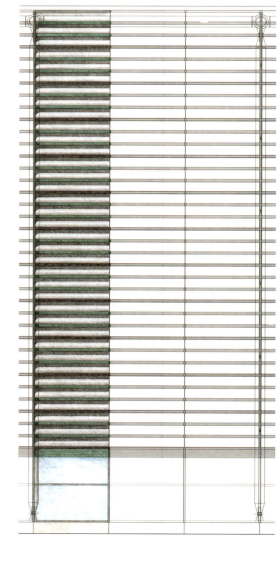

Fassadenschnitt und
Ansicht der Südfassade

Section through façade
and view of south face

Die offene Stellung der Lamellen schafft Transparenz und streut das Licht

The open position of the sunscreen louvres ensures a state of transparency and serves to diffuse daylight

Die Pfosten und Riegelelemente werden mit einer Steckverbindung zusammengefügt. Dabei sind die horizontalen Riegel an den Aufsatzpunkten der Pfosten mit je zwei Bohrungen versehen, so daß die Stege der vertikalen Pfosten mit Stiften verbunden werden können.

Die 12 500 qm große Fläche der Fassaden wurde in der Werkstatt vorgefertigt und endbeschichtet, auf die Baustelle transportiert und vor Ort in 14 Wochen montiert und verglast.

Die gesamte Halle ist rundum verglast. Auf der Innenseite der Fassaden sind dreiteilige Verdunkelungsrollos angebracht, auch die Dachoberlichter können abgedunkelt werden. Die Elemente der Verdunkelung liegen dort im Zwischenraum der Glasscheiben. Die Betonkerne haben Fassaden aus opaken, weißen Glaselementen. Auf der Südseite der Halle wird die gläserne Haut durch feststehende, vorgesetzte Sonnenschutzlamellen gegliedert und vor thermischer Aufheizung geschützt.

of 7.50 m, were designed – in accordance with the flow of forces – with a cross-section resembling a train rail. The rails transmit wind loading to the façade posts. These, in turn, convey the loads partly to the roof and partly to the base slab. The posts and rails have bolted connections. Two holes were bored through the horizontal rails at the points of intersection with the posts to allow the legs of the vertical members to be connected with pins.

The façade, which has an area of 12,500 m², was prefabricated and given its final coating at works. It was subsequently transported to site, erected and glazed within a period of 14 weeks.

All façades of the hall are glazed. A three-part system of blackout blinds was installed on the inside face. The roof lights can also be blacked out. The blackout elements to the roof are located in the cavity between the panes of glass. The external façades to the concrete cores consist of white opaque glass elements. The south face of the hall is articulated by fixed sunscreen louvres on the outside of the glazed skin. These shield the building from solar heat gains.

Ausschnitt aus der Nordfassade mit dem Mittelkern

Detail of south face on middle core

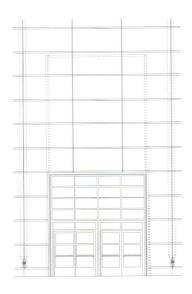
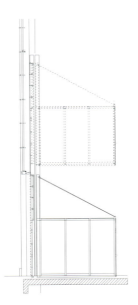
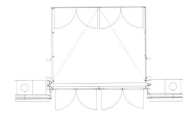

Zur Beschickung der Halle während der Auf- und Abbauphasen sind die Windfänge an der Nordseite der Halle hochfahrbar, um die Durchfahrtshöhe zu gewährleisten.

The entrance lobbies along the north face of the hall can be raised to ensure a maximum opening height for access during the installation and removal phases before and after exhibitions.

Ein- und Anbauten Fitting out and finishings

An der Nordseite der Halle, jeweils am östlichen bzw. westlichen Kern, wurde je ein Restaurant, auf die Allee der vereinigten Bäume gerichtet, situiert, das Restaurant Globus im Westen und die Brasserie im Osten. Beide Restaurants bieten jeweils 250 Personen Platz. Die leichte Stahl-Glas-Konstruktion wurde aus dem Raster der Hallenfassade entwickelt. Die Spannweite von 14 m wird mit Trägern auf Pendelstützen überspannt, die Aussteifung erfolgt über die Dachscheibe aus Holz, die an den Kern angehängt ist. Vor die Fassaden der Restaurants zur Halle hin sind Klappläden aus Holzlamellen gestellt, die außerhalb der Betriebszeiten die Glasfassade schützen. Wenn das Restaurant geöffnet ist, werden die Läden über Seilzüge hochgefahren und bilden ein Vordach für die Sitzplätze vor den Restaurants. Mit der Innenraumgestaltung der Gaststätten war der Innenarchitekt Jan Wichers beauftragt.

Entlang der Westfassade, zwischen nördlichem und südlichem Kern, befindet sich eine 90,00 m lange und 10,50 m breite Galerie. Für die vom Eingang West kommenden Besucher bildet sie den Empfang vor dem Betreten der 12,50 m hohen Halle. Auf der Galerie, die einen guten Überblick über den gesamten Halleninnenraum bietet, stehen 32 m lange Stahlglaskonstruktionen, in denen Büros für Messe- und Veranstaltungszwecke untergebracht sind. Die Galerie ist aus Feuerschutzgründen als Stahlbetonverbundkonstruktion ausgeführt und wird über zwei Freitreppen aus Stahl von der Halle aus erschlossen.

Um einen witterungsunabängigen Hallenrundgang im Messegelände zu ermöglichen, werden alle Hallen durch Übergangsbauwerke untereinander verbunden. Der Übergang zur Halle 12 besteht aus einer 42,50 x 22,50 m großen Stahlkonstruktion mit unterspannten Bogenträgern und eingespannten Stahlstützen. Die Fassaden und das Dach des Verbindungsbaus sind komplett verglast. Die Übergänge werden nicht konditioniert, sie sind jedoch gesprinklert, da sie im Fluchtwegesystem der Hallen 12 und 13 liegen. An den Stirnseiten sind große Schiebetore angeordnet, die die Beschickung der Messehallen während der Auf- und Abbauzeiten sicherstellen.

Two restaurants were installed on the northern side of the hall adjoining the eastern and western cores: the Globus to the west and the Brasserie to the east. Both restaurants seat 250 persons and enjoy views of the Avenue of United Trees. The lightweight steel-and-glass construction was based on the grid dimensions of the hall façade. The restaurant structures, which span a distance of 14 m, consist of girders supported on hinged columns. The structures are braced by rigid timber roofs fixed to the service cores.

Folding timber-louvred shutters to the sides of the restaurants facing the interior of the hall screen the glazed walls when the dining facilities are not in use. When the restaurants are open, the shutters are pulled up by a system of cables and pulleys to form a canopy over the seating outside. The interior design of the restaurants is by Jan Wichers.

Along the west face of the hall, between the northern and southern cores, is a gallery with a length of 90 m and a width of 10.50 m. For visitors approaching from the western entrance, the gallery forms a reception area from where they have a good view over the entire interior, before descending to the 12.50-metre-high hall space. On the gallery are two 32-metre-long steel-and-glass structures. These accommodate offices for trade fair uses and for the various other events held in the hall. For fire-protection reasons, the gallery is in a reinforced concrete composite form of construction. Access to and from the hall is provided via two freestanding steel staircases.

To provide a weather-protected route about the site, covered links will be created between all the halls. The link between Halls 12 and 13 is in the form of a 42.50 x 22.50 m steel structure, consisting of arched girders trussed on the underside and supported by steel columns with rigid fixings. The façades and the roof of this linking tract are fully glazed. These transitional structures will not be air-conditioned, but the link between Halls 12 and 13 does contain a sprinkler system, since it forms part of the escape route network from these spaces. Large sliding gates at the narrow ends allow the halls to be serviced when exhibitions are being assembled and dismantled.

Arbeitsmodell zum Thema Restauranteinbauten

Working model of restaurant structure

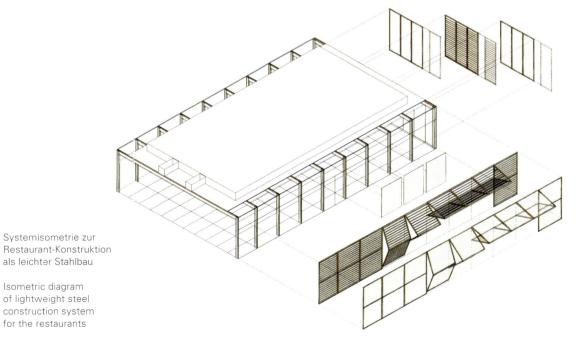

Das Bistro ›Brasserie‹ an der Nordostseite mit den heruntergefahrenen Läden aus Holzlamellen

The Brasserie on the north side with protective timber louvred shutters in a closed position

Systemisometrie zur Restaurant-Konstruktion als leichter Stahlbau

Isometric diagram of lightweight steel construction system for the restaurants

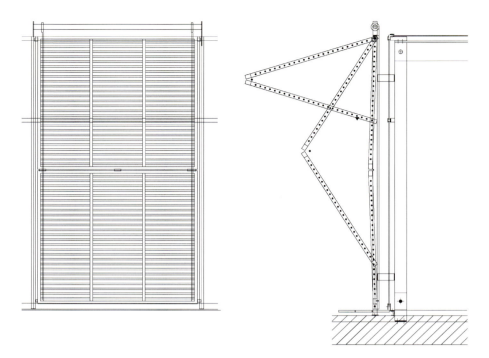

Klappläden vor den Restaurants, die bei Betrieb zu Vordächern hochgefahren werden können

Folding shutters on the outside of the restaurants. During opening hours, the shutters can be raised to form a protective canopy

Restaurantfassade mit geschlossenen Läden aus Rundholzstäben

Restaurant façade with closed shutters consisting of round wood staves

Rechte Seite: Klappläden in den verschiedenen Phasen des Hochfahrens

Opposite page: shutters in various phases of elevation

Raumhoch verglaste Büroräume auf der Galerie an der Westseite

Room-height glazing to offices on gallery along west face of hall

Aus Brandschutzgründen sind die Büroboxer mit einem eigenen Erschließungsflur mit F-30-Verglasung versehen.

As a fire-safety precaution, the office boxes have their own access corridor enclosed in 1/2-hour fire-resistant glazing.

Ansicht der Bürobox mit Anbindung an den Servicekern und hallenseitiger Erschließung über die Freitreppe

Elevation of office box with connection to service core and access to and from hall via free-standing staircase

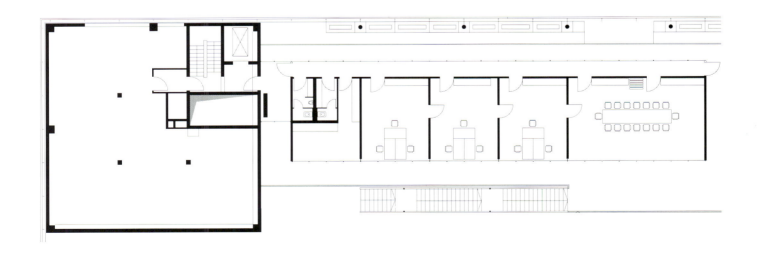

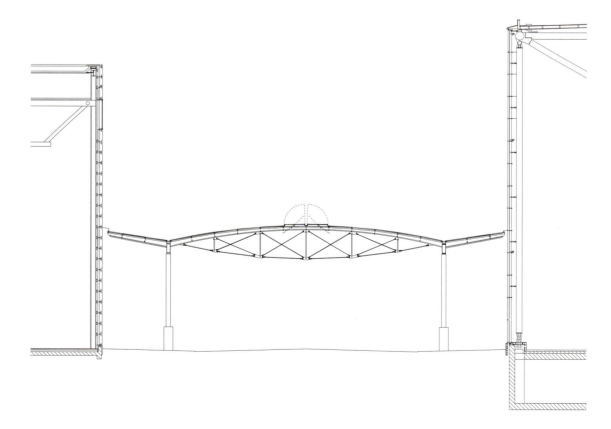

Schnitt durch den Übergang zwischen Halle 12 und Halle 13 mit den filigran unterspannten Stahlbindern

Section through linking tract between Halls 12 and 13 with slenderly dimensioned steel girders trussed on underside

Unten und links:
Übergang von der Halle 12
zur Halle 13 während des
Messebetriebs

Bottom and left:
Linking tract between
Halls 12 and 13 during
a trade fair

Lüftungskonzept
Ventilation concept

Die Auslegung der Lüftungsanlagen für den Hallenbereich erfolgte für 16 000 Personen bei Veranstaltungen und 12 000 Personen bei Messebetrieb. Die Kühllast beträgt 30 W/qm bis max. 65 W/qm äußere und 100 W/qm innere Lasten. Im Winter wird eine Raumtemperatur von 20°C, im Sommer von 22°C bis 28°C angestrebt.

Die Zuluftversorgung erfolgt über ein symmetrisches Kanalsystem, bestehend aus je einem Hauptversorgungskanal entlang der Nord- und Südfassade sowie der achsenweise angeordneten Versorgungskanäle für die Luftauslässe in Ost-West-Richtung. Die Hauptversorgungskanäle Nord und Süd sind über die Versorgungskanäle der Luftauslässe miteinander verbunden. Es ergibt sich ein gemeinsames Kanalsystem über die gesamte Halle, welches von den sechs Zentralgeräten gespeist wird. Auf diese Weise kann über Zu- und Wegschalten einzelner Lüftungsgeräte der Volumenstrom auf ein für den jeweiligen Bedarfsfall notwendiges Minimum reduziert werden.

Die Halle ist in sieben Regelzonen, sechs entlang der Hallenfassaden und eine für den Halleninnenbereich, unabhängig von den Zentralgeräten eingeteilt. Auf diese Weise kann im Winter dem unterschiedlichen Wärmebedarf in den Fassadenbereichen und im Innenbereich der Halle Rechnung getragen werden.

The ventilation installation for the hall was designed for a capacity of 16,000 persons at special events and 12,000 persons attending trade fairs. The external cooling load ranges from 30 W/m² to a maximum of 65 W/m²; the internal cooling load is 100 W/m². In winter, the aim is to maintain an internal temperature of 20°C; the target in summer is a temperature between 22°C and 28°C.

Fresh air is supplied via a symmetrical system of ducts, consisting of a main supply duct along the north and south faces and transverse service ducts with air inlets laid out in an east-west direction along the axes of the hall. The main supply ducts on the north and south sides are linked by the ducts with air inlets. In this way, a universal system was installed over the entire area of the hall, fed by six central units. The volume flow rate can be reduced to a minimum simply by switching individual ventilation units on or off as required.

The hall is divided into seven zones: six along the outer faces of the building and one in the central area. This division is independent of the central units. With this system, it is possible to meet the different winter heating requirements of the peripheral zones and the central zone.

Air is blown in by adjustable rotary fans distributed over the area of the hall. In the zones along the façades, there are additional air inlets, which flush the outer skin with heated air in the areas frequented by people. In this way, a drop in air-temperatures along the façades is prevented.

Ansicht der Hallenwestseite während der Bauzeit

View of west face of hall during construction

Arbeitsmodell zur Abstimmung der Abluftkanäle und Venturiflügel

Working model for adjustment of air-extract ducts and Venturi elements

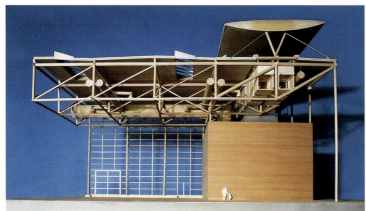

The air inlets themselves can be motor-operated to respond to temperature changes. Heated air, for example, can be blown vertically downwards; or alternatively, cooled air can be blown out horizontally. The different directions of air injection take account of the difference between the density of the air supply and that of the air in the hall, thereby ensuring a good mixture of the two and avoiding any sensation of draughts.

Sixty per cent of the exhaust air is extracted from the hall via the continuous plinth zone around the façade, along the escape tunnels, through a circular duct system at lower-floor level and up vertical shafts in the service cores. The remaining 40 per

Die Zuluft wird über verstellbare Drallauslässe, welche flächig über die Halle verteilt sind, in dieselbe eingeblasen. In den Fassadenbereichen wurde die Anzahl der Luftauslässe erhöht, um die gesamte Fassade im Aufenthaltsbereich mit erwärmter Zuluft bestreichen und somit den Kaltluftabfall verhindern zu können.

Die Luftauslässe selbst sind in Abhängigkeit der Temperatur motorisch verstelbar, so daß erwärmte Luft vertikal nach unten bzw. gekühlte Luft horizontal ausgeblasen werden kann. Die unterschiedlichen Ausblasrichtungen tragen der unterschiedlichen Dichte der Zuluft im Vergleich zur Raumluft Rechnung und sorgen so für eine gute Durchmischung der Raumluft mit Zuluft unter Vermeidung von Zugerscheinungen.

Die Abluft der Halle wird zu ca. 60 % im umlaufenden Sockelbereich der Fassade und der Fluchttunnel über ein Ringkanalsystem im Untergeschoß mit entsprechenden Steigschächten in den Servicekernen und zu 40 % an der Decke abgesaugt.

Zur natürlichen Absaugung wurden über den Servicekernen auf dem Hallendach sechs Tragflächenprofile, sogenannte Venturiflügel, gebaut. Bei Anströmung durch Wind bildet sich durch die Querschnittsverringerung unter den Profilen und die damit verbundene Geschwindigkeitserhöhung der durchströmenden Luft ein Unterdruck, der die Abluft durch eine entsprechende Öffnung im Hallendach unter dem Venturiflügel aus der Halle saugt. Die Öffnung ist in der Halle mit je zwei Kästen (sog. Venturikanäle), Querschnitt je 2 x 2 m, auf

cent of the exhaust air is extracted via ceiling outlets. Six wing-like structures or "Venturi elements" were erected on the roof of the hall over the service cores to create a natural suction effect that is exploited to extract vitiated air from the interior. Wind currents over the roof flow through the constricted space beneath these elements, which results in an increased wind velocity. This, in turn, causes a state of vacuum that is exploited to suck vitiated air from the hall through the respective roof openings beneath the Venturi elements. Attached to the openings are two trunking units ("Venturi ducts")

Venturiflügel mit V-Stützen aus Rundrohren und Abspannung

Venturi element with V-shape tubular supports and diagonal stays

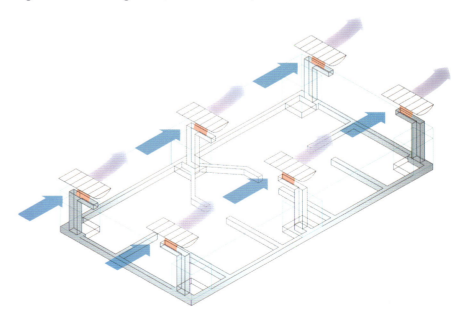

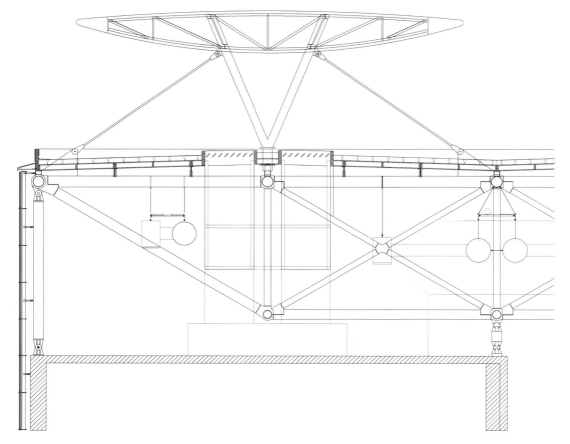

Schnitt durch Abluftkanal und Venturiflügel

Section through air-extract duct and Venturi element

Abluftkanal im Dachtragwerk unter der Dacheindeckung

Air-extract duct in roof structure beneath covering

Abluftöffnungen unter dem Venturiflügel mit Klappenmechanismus zur Steuerung der Luftmengen

Exhaust outlets beneath Venturi elements, with flap mechanism to control the air-flow volume

25 m Länge versehen, die sowohl über die Abluftschächte in den Servicekernen mit dem Ringkanalsystem im Untergeschoß als auch über Jalousieklappen mit dem Deckenbereich der Halle direkt in Verbindung stehen.

Eine Untersuchung des Tragflächenprofiles am Institut für Industrieaerodynamik der FH Aachen hat die Funktionsweise im Rahmen der Planung bestätigt. Hierbei hat sich ergeben, daß das natürliche Abluftsystem zu 45 % des Jahres einen ausreichenden Volumenstrom selbst bei einer Außenluftrate von 100 % sicherstellt. Bei einer Außenluftrate von 40 % (Minimum) erreicht das natürliche Abluftsystem eine Verfügbarkeit von 70%. Die Verfügbarkeit wurde sogar übertroffen.

Die Öffnungen unter dem Venturiflügel selbst sind mit Klappen versehen, die sich, um die unterschiedlichen Windgeschwindigkeiten und den damit variierenden Unterdruck unter dem Flügelprofil ausregeln zu können, in Abhängigkeit vom Unterdruck in den Venturikanälen öffnen und schließen.

Die Venturikanäle sind bis an die Fassade herangezogen und besitzen Axialventilatoren, um die Abluftabsaugung bei zu geringen Windgeschwindigkeiten oder bei Windstille zu gewährleisten.

Das Abluftkanalsystem ist, um die Unterdrücke des natürlichen Abluftsystems umsetzen zu können, mit Strömungsgeschwindigkeiten von 1,5 m/s im Ringkanal bzw. den Fluchttunneln und 3 m/s in den Steigschächten dimensioniert.

Volker Vomhoff

2 x 2 m in cross-section and 25 m long. The trunking units are directly linked, via the extract shafts in the service cores, to the duct circuit system at lower-floor level and, via louvred flaps, to the ceiling outlets in the hall.

Investigations of the cross-sectional form of the wing-like structures (Venturi elements) carried out at the Institute for Industrial Aerodynamics of the College of Higher Education in Aachen confirmed the functional efficiency of these structures in the context of the project planning. It was shown that for 45 per cent of the year, the natural ventilation system would guarantee an adequate volume flow rate even when the intake of external air was 100 per cent. With minimal external air movements and a 40 per cent air intake, the natural air extract system achieves a 70-per-cent level of serviceability. Under certain conditions, it was possible even to exceed this figure.

The openings beneath the Venturi elements are fitted with movable flaps that open and close according to different wind speeds and the resulting vacuum changes beneath the elements, thereby regulating the flow of air.

The Venturi ducts themselves extend out to the façade and are equipped with axial fans that ensure an adequate air extract when the external wind speed is too low.

In order to exploit the vacuum conditions for the natural extraction of vitiated air, the system of extract ducts is dimensioned to ensure an air-flow rate of 1.5 m/s in the duct circuit and the escape tunnels and 3 m/s in the vertical shafts.

Volker Vomhoff

Computersimulationen zur Tageslichtverteilung vom Fraunhofer Institut für Solare Energiesysteme

Computer simulations of daylight distribution carried out by the Fraunhofer Institute for Solar Energy Systems

Beleuchtungsprobe vor Fertigstellung der Halle

Lighting trials before completion of hall

Deckenspiegel mit
Aufteilung der natürlicher und künstlichen Beleuchtung

Underside of roof showing layout of roof lights and artificial lighting installation

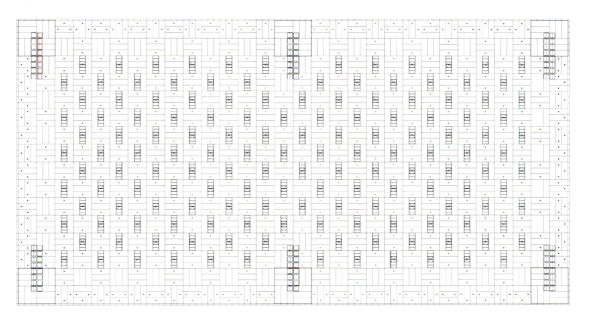

Messenutzung der Halle 13 während der Cebit 1998

Hall 13 in use during the 1998 Cebit trade fair

Halle mit eingestellter Tribüne für Konzertveranstaltungen

Hall with a stage built in for concerts

Die ATP-Tennisweltmeisterschaft in der Halle 13

The ATP World Tennis Championships in Hall 13

**Projektbeteiligte
Persons and organizations involved in the project**

Bauherr
Client
Deutsche Messe AG, Hannover
Expo 2000 Hannover GmbH

Architekten
Architects
Ackermann und Partner, München
Kurt Ackermann, Peter Ackermann
Projektpartner/Project partner:
Peter Ackermann
Mitarbeiter/Assistants
Ying Chang, Hannelore Huber,
Barbara Karl, Beate Kuntz,
Herbert Markert, Reiner Nagel,
Susanne Nobis, Dagmar Plankemann,
Horst Raab, Heinz Riegel

Tragwerksplanung, Wettbewerb
Structural engineers, competition
Christoph Ackermann
und Dr. Bernhard Behringer, München

Peter Ackermann, rechts, im Gespräch mit einem Mitarbeiter. Unten: Baustellenbesuch des Architekturbüros Ackermann und Partner

Peter Ackermann, right speaking with a colleague. Below: Architectural firm Ackermann and Parnter visiting the construction site

Planung und Ausführung
Planning and realization
Schlaich, Bergermann und Partner, Stuttgart
Projektleitung/Project supervision
Sven Plieninger
Mitarbeiter/Assistants
Christoph Ackermann, Frauke Fluhr,
Thorsten Helbig

Betonkonstruktionen
Concrete structures
Renk, Horstmann, Renk, Laatzen
Projektleitung / Project supervision
Franz-Josef Ameling

Prüfstatik
Structural control office
Prof. Dr. Stein, Hannover

Haustechnik
Mechanical services
Fischer Energie und Haustechnik Consult,
Wehrheim, Siegfried Fischer
Mitarbeiter/Assistants
Volker Vomhoff, Heinrich Kasdorf

Künstlerische Oberleitung und
Objektüberwachung
Overall artistic direction and supervision of project
Ackermann und Partner, München
Harms und Partner, Hannover
Mitarbeiter / Assistants
Christian Danner, Christoph Güttler,
Rainer Konrad, Claus Mansbrügge

Tages- und Kunstlichtsimulation
Daylight and artificial lighting simulation
Fraunhofer Institut für Solare Energiesysteme
ISE, Freiburg, Dr. Manuel Goller

Windkanalversuche
Wind-tunnel tests
Institut für Industrieaerodynamik, FH Aachen

Projektsteuerung
Project management
Assmann Beraten + Planen GmbH, Braunschweig
Projektleitung/Project supervision
Dr. Wolfgang Henning
Mitarbeiter / Assistant
Horst Bleßmann

Innenarchitektur der Restaurants
Restaurant interior design
Studio Jan Wichers, Hamburg

Grundsteinlegung.
Sepp D. Heckmann,
Dr. Ing. Theodor Wuppermann,
Theodor Diener,
Oberbürgermeister Herbert Schmalstieg.
Hubert H. Lange

Laying the cornerstone.
Sepp D. Heckmann,
Dr. Ing. Theodor Wuppermann,
Mayor Herbert Schmalstieg,
Hubert H. Lange

Dr. Rainar Herbertz,
Sepp D. Heckmann.
Prof. Dr. Kurt Ackermann
auf der Baustelle

Dr. Rainar Herbertz,
Sepp D. Heckmann.
Prof. Dr. Kurt Ackermann
at the construction site

Peter Ackermann bei der
Einweihung der Halle 13

Peter Ackermann at
the opening ceremony
for Hall 13

Technische Daten
Technical data

Außenmaße der Halle (Länge x Breite)
226,26 m x 121,26 m
Lichte Höhe ü. OKF EG   12,80 m
Max. Höhe   18,60 m
Venturiflügel   22,50 x 12,50 m; max. Höhe über Gelände   23,30 m
Größte Stützenfreiheit   225 x 120 m
Überbaute Fläche   27 433 m²
Umbauter Raum   525 135 m³
Bruttofläche nach FKM   24 480 m²
Glasfassade   12 530 m²
Erdbewegung   80 500 m³
Schalung   48 800 m²
Stahlbeton   15 700 m³
Betonstahl   2 365 t

Stahlmassen   2 810 t
Belastbarkeit des Hallenbodens   100 kN/m²
Heizleistung   4,9 MW
Kälteleistung   4,4 MW
Lüftung inkl. Nebenanlagen   740 000 m³/h
Elektroversorgung   6 Trafos x 1 250 KW
Beleuchtung, mittl. Beleuchtungsstärke im Ausstellungsbereich   300 LUX
Elektrische Ausstellerversorgung   300 W/m²
Gaststätten-Anzahl Plätze   2 x 276
Snacks   2
Toilettenanlagen Damen/Herren/Behinderten-WC   3/3/2
Lasten- und Personenaufzüge   3

External dimensions of hall (length x width) 226.26 x 121.26 m
Clear height above FFL   12.80 m
Max. height   18.60 m
Venturi elements   22.50 x 12.50 m; max. height above site   23.30 m
Max. column-free area   225 x 120 m
Area of building (footprint)   27,433 m²
Gross volume   525,135 m³
Gross area (standard calculation for trade fair structures)   24,480 m²
Glass façade   12,530 m
Excavation and infill   80,500 m³
Formwork   48,800 m²
Reinforced concrete   15,700 m³

Steel reinforcement   2,365 t
Steel structure   2,810 t
Load-bearing capacity of hall floor   100 kN/m²
Heating capacity   4.9 MW
Cooling capacity   4.4 MW
Ventilation, incl. ancillary plant   740,000 m³/h
Electrical supply   6 transformers x 1,250 KW
Lighting (mean lighting intensity in exhibition areas)   300 lux
Electrical supply for exhibitors   300 W/m²
Restaurant seating   2 x 276
Snack bars   2
Toilet facilities (women/men/disabled)   3/3/2
Goods and passenger lifts   3

Impressum

© Prestel Verlag, München · London · New York, und Ackermann und Partner, München, 1999

Wenn nicht anders angegeben, stammen die Texte von Ackermann und Partner, Malsenstraße 57, 80638 München

Auf dem Umschlag: Halleninnenraum nach Westen
Foto: Richie Müller, München

Die Deutsche Bibliothek – CIP-Einheitsaufnahme
Ackermann und Partner < München >
Halle 13 : Expo-Halle ; Expo 2000 GmbH ;
Deutsche Messe AG, Hannover / Ackermann und
Partner. Hrsg. von Peter Ackermann. Vorw. von
Sepp D. Heckmann. – München ; London ;
New York : Prestel, 1999
ISBN 3-7913-2018-1

Prestel Verlag · Mandlstraße 26 · 80802 München
Tel. 089/381709-0 · Fax 089/381709-35

Redaktionelle Mitarbeit: Horst Raab
Lektorat: Katharina Wurm
Satz und Gestaltung: Norbert Dinkel, München
Reproduktionen: Reproline, München
Druck: Aumüller Druck, Regensburg
Bindung: Gassenmeyer, Nürnberg

Gedruckt auf chlorfrei gebleichtem Papier

Printed in Germany
ISBN 3-7913-2018-1

© Prestel Verlag, Munich · London · New York, and Ackermann and Partners, Munich, 1999

Unless otherwise stated all texts were written by Ackermann and Partners, Malsenstrasse 57, D-80638 Munich

Translated from the German by Peter Green

Cover: Interior of hall looking to the west
Photo: Richie Müller, Munich

Library of Congress Cataloging-in-Publication Data is available

Prestel Verlag · Mandlstrasse 26 · D-80802 Munich
Tel. +49 (89) 381709-0; Fax +49 (89) 381709-35;
16 West 22nd Street · New York, NY 10010 USA
Tel. +001 (212) 627-9090 · Fax +001 (212) 627-9511;
and 4 Bloomsbury Place · London WC1A 2QA
Tel. +44 (0171) 323 5004 · Fax +44 (0171) 636 8004

Prestel books are available worldwide.
Please contact your nearest bookseller or write to one of the above addresses for information concerning your local distributor.

Editing: Horst Raab, Katharina Wurm
Typesetting and Design: Norbert Dinkel, Munich
Lithography: Reproline, Munich
Printing: Aumüller Druck, Regensburg
Binding: Gassenmeyer, Nürnberg

Printed in Germany
ISBN 3-7913-2018-1

Fotonachweis
Photo credits

Peter Ackermann   27 (oben u. rechts), 61 (oben u. rechts)
Aerophot Demuss   5, 24
Christian Gahl   2, 15, 18/19, 20, 22, 23, 29, 31 (unten), 33, 34, 35, 52/53, 62/63
Frîa Hagen   12/13, 14, 36, 42, 49, 50, 51, 55, 59 (unten), 61 (Mitte)
Erhard Heidenreich   61 (unten)
Frank Höreth   58 (oben u. Mitte), 59 (Mitte), 60
Maximilian Hüller   59 (oben)
Richie Müller   Umschlag, 21, 25, 37, 38/39, 41, 43, 44, 45, 46, 47, 56/57
Reiner Nagel   26, 27 (unten), 48 (oben)
Horst Raab   6, 11, 32, 40, 48 (unten),
Jürgen Schmidt-Lohmann   58 (unten)
Jens Weber   16/17, 31 (oben)

Modellbau / Model design
Seite 6, 11, 40 und 48   Ackermann und Partner
Seite 32   Atelier Hönigschmidt, München